The Work and Office
of an
Evangelist

David Sanderson

Church Army
Evangelist and Evangelism Adviser

GROVE BOOKS LIMITED
BRAMCOTE NOTTINGHAM NG9 3DS

Contents

Acknowledgements
Many thanks to all the evangelists who answered questions and provided the stories.
Names have been changed to preserve anonymity.

The Cover Illustration is by Peter Ashton

First Impression August 1995
ISSN 0953-4946
ISBN 1 85174 297 2

1
Introduction

Two full-time evangelists had been invited to lead a meeting with a view to encouraging members of a congregation to witness to their faith in Christ. About twelve people attended the meeting. The evangelists began by telling their own faith story to the group. When they had finished they invited others present to tell their stories. A response came from Mary, an elderly lady tucked insignificantly in the corner. She spoke for a few minutes about the fact that the Lord was with her and answered her prayers. The evangelists tried hard to get the rest of the group to speak, but without much success until one of them asked if there were particular people who had helped those present on their way to faith in Christ. John, an older man, spoke and said there was one person, but as that person was in the room he did not want to mention a name. However, when pressed, he named Mary, the elderly lady in the corner. Pat, a young woman, was next. 'I would have to say the same, it is Mary who has helped me.' And so it went on. Almost everyone in that group identified Mary as the one person, more than any other, who had helped them on their pilgrimage to faith. What the visiting evangelists realized was that there was already another evangelist present who through her prayers and witness was leading folk into a knowledge of God.

John was in his early twenties, a chemistry teacher at the local high school and in his spare time a youth leader in his local church. He was excited about the way Jesus had changed his life and wanted to share his faith with others. However, it was as a youth leader that this desire was best fulfilled. He had a knack for getting alongside the teenagers and over a period of time he helped a number of them to find a personal relationship with Jesus. He did, of course, sometimes speak at the youth meetings, but most of his work was done in one-to-one conversations with individuals.

Betty was a peripatetic hairdresser working in the rural area around where she lived. Although a churchgoer for some time, her faith did not come alive until she attended a Billy Graham meeting and responded to the gospel. She wanted to tell others about her new experience of God. As she went about her work travelling from house to house she had a ready-made network of people whom she knew and with whom she conversed regularly. So as and when opportunity arose she spoke about Jesus and invited her customers to follow Christ.

2
Who are the Evangelists?

These people were not recognized by the church as evangelists and would hardly have described themselves as such. Yet they were witnessing to the good news and seeing others moving closer to God through their message. If we describe such people as evangelists, and I believe we should, then we are suggesting something different from what most people think of as an evangelist. There are certain stereotypes, like that of the itinerant preacher. Yet evangelists come in all shapes and sizes. In fact, most evangelists are not up-front preachers at all, but very ordinary folk sharing the gospel in natural ways with those they meet. If this is so, then we need a fresh understanding. We must therefore ask, what is an evangelist?

New Testament Evangelizers
In trying to answer this question we shall first look to the Bible for clues. The term 'evangelist' (Greek: *euangelistes)* occurs only three times in the New Testament (Acts 21.8; Eph 4.11; 2 Tim 4.5), but it does not follow these are the only places where evangelists are mentioned. The word is closely related to two other terms, 'gospel' or 'good news' (Greek: *euangelion)* and 'to preach the good news' (Greek: *euangelizomai).* The most natural inference from these words is that an evangelist has something to do with the telling of the good news of Jesus. There were many people in the New Testament, not least the apostles, who were preaching the gospel and therefore fulfilling the role of evangelist, even though they were not so named.

There is also the ministry of the one named evangelist in the Bible, Philip (Acts 21.8). He was one of seven men, full of the Holy Spirit, set apart to help with the administration of finance in the Jerusalem church, so that the apostles could give themselves to prayer and the ministry of the word (Acts 6.1-6), that is, teaching and evangelism. Philip is represented as one of a number of believers who after the persecution of the Jerusalem church 'went everywhere, preaching the message' (Acts 8.4) and eventually some of them 'went as far as Phoenicia, Cyprus and Antioch' while others 'went to Antioch and proclaimed the message to Gentiles...and a great number of people believed' (Acts 11.19-20). These people were doing the work of evangelists. The actual designation 'evangelist' probably came later as ministry became a little more settled.[1]

---

1   The fact that Philip is not called an evangelist until later in Acts (21.8) and that the word occurs in Ephesians and 2 Timothy may support this view. In Acts and even more sharply in Ephesians the evangelist's function is identified over against and yet complementary to that of the apostles and the other named ministries.

Philip himself eventually reached Samaria. There he proclaimed Christ, performed miraculous signs, exorcized evil spirits and people believed (Acts 8.4-8). He appears to have planted a church, for it is recorded, 'when they believed Philip as he preached the good news of the kingdom of God and the name of Jesus Christ, they were baptized' (Acts 8.9-25). At the command of an angel, he left what seems to have been a successful work and engaged in one-to-one evangelism (8.26-39). He also exercises a mobile ministry until he reaches Caesarea, where he is still residing some dozen or so years later (Acts 8.40; 21.8). We simply have a glimpse of Philip which offers us a picture of the ministry of one evangelist. Yet this picture will help in our search for clues about the work of an evangelist.[2]

It would appear, then, that an evangelist is concerned with the communication of the gospel of the kingdom or reign of God to those who have not received it. In the case of Philip we have a pioneer ministry. He preaches the gospel, plants a new church in Samaria and shares the gospel with an Ethiopian. The ministry also included healing and exorcism. According to F S Spencer, 'The most cogent hypothesis conceives of evangelists as missionaries who proclaim the gospel just like the apostles and prophets but who could not, with Paul and the Twelve, lay claim to a direct commission from Christ and to the immediate revelation of the gospel by the Spirit.'[3]

In seeking to answer our question as to the function of the evangelist we must be careful not to give a one-sided view. It is much too easy to think of an evangelist as having a solo ministry which has little connection with the continuing life of the church. Yet such a view of an evangelist would be at variance with good practice and the picture offered in the Bible.

Evangelist in the Church Community

Next, then, let us consider some illustrations of good practice. An Anglican 'community evangelist' stresses the importance of his relationship with the church in his work with the Muslims. The church and the three mosques are working together to improve the quality of life in the area, so good relationships between the two faith communities have been established. Even though known as 'the missionary' by some of the Muslims, this evangelist is respected by them because he has a recognized leadership role in the local church. At least a part of his credibility with the Muslim community arises from the way the church community, of which he is a member, has co-operated in social action with the mosques. Working within a framework of Muslim-Christian friendships he has been able from time to time to invite those present in the mosque to explore the meaning of passages of the Bible.

---

2   The picture of Philip is shaped by the way Luke develops the story of the stages in the spread of the word of God. See F S Spencer, *The Portrait of Philip in Acts* (Sheffield University, 1992).
3   *Ibid* p 262.

The role of the evangelist-in-church-in-local-community is crucial in this situation.

While the focus in this example is on a particular situation, it makes the point from the sharp end. Such an understanding of the evangelist's relationship to the church is crucial in most, if not all, situations and especially for an evangelist working in a local church. The credibility of the church and the evangelist hang together. They need each other. In fact, one evangelist rightly warned that evangelists are open to many dangers if they operate as 'lone rangers.' They need to be appointed and sent.

A Free Church itinerant evangelist was describing his work. Part of his ministry, he said, was to help churches take evangelism seriously. He explained how when he visits a church to set up an evangelism project he first shows the church members how to do whatever kind of evangelism is appropriate for them. Then he makes sure that by the time the initial project is finished he has provided sufficient training and support for them to carry on with the evangelism as a part of their continuing mission. In so training and enabling church members in evangelism this evangelist is not alone. Many evangelists today say that working with and enabling the church in evangelism is an important part of their work. Evangelists work with the church to the advantage of both.

Such understandings of the work of an evangelist fit with Ephesians 4.11ff. The passage offers a list of five ministry functions: apostles, prophets, evangelists, pastors and teachers. Apostles and prophets are foundational members of the church (Eph 2.20) who have been given a special gift of the Spirit as vehicles of God's revelation (Eph 3.5). Pastors and teachers can be taken as two aspects of the same office. These ministries are given 'for the equipment of the saints, for the work of ministry, for building up the body of Christ.'[4] While Ephesians recognizes the importance of the church as the primary evangelizing agency, it has no difficulty with the existence of a distinctive ministry function of 'evangelists.' Evangelists here are viewed as members of a community of ministers who enable the church to fulfil its role.

How far is this also true of the picture of Philip the evangelist? He was a member of the Jerusalem Christian community, under the leadership of the apostles and a member of a team of seven. He left Jerusalem under pressure of persecution, so there may not have been a formal 'sending,' as with Paul and Barnabas (Acts 13.1ff). He established a gospel community in Samaria and Jerusalem apostles visit Samaria to affirm his work. The whole operation takes place within the network of community relationships.

---

4   The metaphor 'building up' is also used in Ephesians 2.20-21 of the temple under construction, or not yet completed. This suggests a ministry to those who are not yet believers, those yet to be built into the community of faith.

There are, however, some questions regularly raised about the relationship of evangelists to the church and we must try to answer them. Do evangelists detract from the evangelistic effectiveness of the local church? We must admit that congregations are frequently content to let the specialist evangelists do the work for them, but this ought not to be the case. The continuing lifestyle and witness of a local congregation are essential ingredients in evangelism. There is often good reason to invite a specialist evangelist to help with evangelism. In these cases evangelists will contribute to the effectiveness of the local church. Yet specialists will not be very effective if they do not have the continuing work of the church to build on. Some kind of partnership is required.

Should we not be concentrating on enabling the whole church to witness rather than encouraging evangelists? The author of Ephesians would probably answer that the church should be doing both, and with this we agree. Not all evangelists are itinerants. Many are members of local congregations and as such provide a focus for evangelism in the local church seeking to stimulate vision for evangelism, being a training resource, working with church members and helping the church identify other evangelists. If in a congregation potential evangelists can be identified and set free for evangelism, then surely this is the church doing evangelism. Further, an evangelist can encourage the church members in their daily witness. If such an evangelist is part of the leadership team, then there is an overlap with all the other functions of the church. In such circumstances worship, prayer, teaching, serving can all develop an evangelistic element and vice versa.

Yet we also need to remember that evangelists often feel marginalized by the church. Churches, at times, fail to support them, especially as their work is with people who are not yet Christians. A church can put pressure on by expecting too much too soon, or can ignore them altogether. Any group of new Christians they may gather together may not easily fit into existing church structures and the church may not be prepared to make the necessary adjustments. The ministry of John Wesley and the emergence of the Methodist Church stand as a reminder of Anglican inflexibility in the face of effective evangelism.

What Then is an Evangelist?

Several things may now be said in attempting to define the role of the evangelist. First, there is the task of making contact with and leading people into the gospel community for the first time. If the evangelist does not have an 'audience' with whom to communicate, then there can be no evangelism. In the New Testament the gospel preacher 'finds' a group of people who have not heard or only partially understood the message. Therefore it would seem that the evangelist cannot avoid at least some responsibility for helping to create the audience of unbelievers. In churches where there is a dynamic

7

Christian community life one would expect such a group to already be in existence and available to the evangelist. Yet the fact remains that in many situations this will be an essential part of the evangelist's role.

Second, Philip the evangelist preached 'the good news of the kingdom of God and the name of Jesus.' A comparison of the ministry of Philip with that of Jesus may be helpful. Three things in the ministry of Jesus may offer a model. He called people into the community which served the kingdom. He was concerned about the marginalized and the 'sinner.' And he released people from disabilities and pressures which trapped them. Clearly, Philip's evangelism is akin to this.[5]

However, there is a shift in focus from Jesus to Philip. For Philip, Jesus is not only the model for his ministry but also the message. Philip's message was about 'the Christ' (Acts 8.5), 'the good news of the Kingdom of God and name of Jesus Christ' (Acts 8.12), 'the good news of Jesus' (Acts 8.35). Integral to the proclamation of the kingdom of God, the story of Jesus has to be told. The good news about Jesus is central to the proclamation of the kingdom of God, whether by an evangelist or any other.

The gospel message touches the lives of individuals but has much wider implications. In Philip's case it brings physical healing and release as well as a joyous reception of the message. Once an evangelist proclaims 'Christ is Lord' they are committed to understanding the evangel which impinges upon the context and culture of the lives of those they are seeking to evangelize. The evangelist will, as appropriate to time and place, have to say and do things about the context in which life is set, especially where context and culture dehumanize or enslave people. If evangelism is about repentance and change, it goes beyond the individual and includes the need for communities also to repent and change.

Third, and arising directly out of the idea of the universal reign of God, evangelists are pioneers. They break new ground with the gospel. As each new community, segment of society or individual hears the good news for the first time so the rule of God becomes evident in new places and contexts. As new people respond so the light of the gospel is reflected in new ways.

Fourth, the community aspect of evangelists' ministry is important. The church recognizes their special gift for communicating the gospel and sends them with its authority to extend the kingdom of God. Sometimes they will start new gospel communities in places where there are none. Such communities are an integral expression of God's reign and are committed by their very nature to the full implication of that reign in the world. Evangelists also have a role within the church. They are a focus for evangelism, pioneering initiatives, training and enabling church members to witness and identifying potential evangelists.

---

5   We can see this even though we have a much briefer account of Philip's ministry.

No evangelist will do all the things suggested above at the same time but if we are seeking to identify the role we must embrace all these aspects.

An evangelist, then, is a member of the Christian community, an agent for change and a pioneer in and a focus for evangelism. An evangelist takes initiatives in communicating the story of Jesus to those who are not Christian believers. He or she will apply that story in ways appropriate to the particular situation, call for a Christ-centred change in the lives of the hearers and invite them to enter the gospel community.[6] The evangelist cannot be held finally responsible for the consequences of this communication. On the one hand, it could result in far reaching moral change both to individuals and communities. On the other hand, it is possible that people may reject what is put forward or simply want more time to think about the implications of the message.

---

6   Herein lies the key point of difference between an evangelist and a witness. The witness also has a story to tell, but it is the story of the way in which God has touched their life.

3
What Kind of Evangelists Do We Need Today?

Having outlined something the work of an evangelist we ought to ask, 'What kind of evangelists do we need in the UK today?' In asking this question we are not rejecting all that has happened before. For example, evangelists who can explain the gospel clearly or those who gossip the gospel and work in one-to-one situations will always be required. The need for people to establish new churches remains a priority. Some styles stand the test of time; other styles which may not fit the present will, no doubt, reappear in the future.

In responding to this question there is no way a comprehensive answer can be given, but perhaps some flavours will suffice. The stereotype of evangelist as itinerant preacher is misleading. A better basic model is that of an evangelist as one with an informal circle of people around her, whom she is in the process of discipling. This model has been a basic model for a long time but is often overlooked. Further, it fits well with the illustrations of evangelists already offered. It allows flexible dialogue and affirms that evangelists can work in the everyday secular world of work, leisure, community or home. Further, if the church is to make any impact in today's world then we need to encourage, train and enable evangelists to exercise their gifts in such contexts. Such an understanding of an evangelist does not exclude the itinerant preacher nor prescribe a particular method.

More attention must be paid to the evangelist-in-church-in-community approach, mentioned above. David Sherwin's work in which a large part of a congregation at Conisbrough was stimulated to pray and witness offers another example.[7] Elsewhere, an evangelist working with the *Evangelism Explosion* programme has trained a large team of church members in evangelism and they follow up their church's local casual contacts. Over a period of time this work has added significantly to the worshipping congregation.

Some evangelists are in secular occupations and we need more of them. Can we find ways of supporting evangelists in the workplace? One evangelist who worked in a factory prayed regularly for all his workmates and sought opportunities, through friendship, to share with people about Jesus. There was the necessity, he discovered, to develop apologetic skills and lifestyle had to tell. Yet he required further skills and insight to help make a qualitative difference to life in the workplace. In encouraging and training these evangelists we must remember this dimension of their life.

---

7   David R Sherwin, *A Prayer-Evangelism Strategy,* (Grove Evangelism Series No 26, Nottingham: Grove Books, 1994).

Meeting and Communication

With the availability of a variety of means of visual communication, fresh approaches to evangelism are open to us. Two illustrations will suffice to make the point. I watched someone dressed as a puppet lead an open-air meeting, involve passers-by in the action and create opportunities for Christians to talk informally with interested people. I have sat through a multi-media presentation of music, drama, chat, video tracks and a short talk as people were invited to reflect on the good news in a world full of suffering. We need more evangelists who are skilled in audio-visual and participatory evangelism if we are to be effective in up-front and open-air presentations.

We need evangelists who can set up meeting points between church and community. One evangelist set up two informal groups for unchurched teenagers, in her home and in a church hall. Within the context of friendship they discussed almost anything they wanted. The same woman, a mother of four, found the elderly claiming they could not get to church services on Sunday because family visiting. She organized a midweek worship service and no less than forty of these elderly people attended. The gap between the church and the world is wide and we must meet people where they are.

An evangelist, church planting in an Urban Priority Area, found it impossible to ignore the call to preach the gospel to the marginalized. Here in Britain today is another aspect of life which cannot be ignored. Many people are marginalized and need very practical help. The evangelist mentioned saw his role not only as leading people to faith, but as bringing about social change. Evangelists with a prophetic vision who can relate the gospel to the wider issues of life are required by the church today.

A large mission had been arranged and various preachers had been invited to explain the gospel to those who were to attend. In the main the evangelistic speakers came with expositions of biblical texts supported by Christian 'in jokes,' most of which would have been lost on non-Christians present. Only one evangelist made any serious attempt to cross the culture divide between church and secular community. He began his address, 'When I was in the pub the other night…' which was anathema to some of the Christians present. He went on to talk about various understandings of love, using popular vocabulary. He slowly lead people to think about the love of God revealed in Jesus. The church is set in a secular world and we need to be able to communicate good news within that terminology.

We cannot either overlook the current interest in small group evangelism popularized through *Good News Down the Street* and *Alpha* courses. Many evangelists are using these programmes as they recognize that people coming to faith today need time to think through the implications of the faith. Alongside these programmes there is the renewed interest in the catechumenate, which with its liturgical rites has an added dimension that affirms the evangelist-in-church-in-community concept.

4

Evangelists in the Church of England

Having explored something of the function of the evangelist we shall now ask, 'How do evangelists fit into the Church of England?'

The Bishop's Evangelistic Role

The evangelist's role has been given some attention in the ordering of bishops. The consecration of bishops in the 1662 *Book of Common Prayer* includes a prayer that the new bishop 'may evermore be ready to spread abroad thy Gospel, the glad tiding of reconciliation with thee.' The 1980 *Alternative Service Book* (ASB) includes the following words: '[the bishop] is to promote [the Church's] mission throughout the world…He is to have special care for the outcast and the needy; and to those who turn to God he is to declare forgiveness of sins.' Bishops are also asked to affirm that they will be 'a faithful witness to Christ to those among whom [they] live, and lead [their] people to obey our Saviour's commands to make disciples of all nations.'

Perhaps we can say two things about these statements. First, they reflect a theology of the transmission of authority. Our Lord Jesus Christ exercised authority as he obediently did the work of his Father. He gave authority to the church through his apostles and disciples who followed him (Matt 16.19; 18.18; Acts 3.6). Whatever the exercise of this authority in New Testament times, it became focused in the ordained ministry, and, in particular, in the person of the bishop who among other things embodied the local church's relationship with the wider church. John Goldingay writes:

> 'There is still something in the equation of apostle and (modern style) bishop. Paul was aware that he was a means whereby the links between geographically separate churches received expression. In teaching, in news, in mutual support they were one through him. There is a sense here in which a bishop can still exercise the authority of the apostles.'[8]

Second, if the Christian ministry within a diocese comes under the authority of the bishop and is derived from him, then part of his role was, for a long time, underplayed. The pastoral and caring ministry has been carried on by priests and deacons, but the focus on evangelism was missing. A change came with the ASB, where deacons are among other things 'to…search out the careless and the indifferent…' and priests are to 'proclaim the word of

---

8 John Goldingay, *Authority in Ministry*, (Grove Worship Series No 46, Nottingham: Grove Books, 1976) p 20.

the Lord, to call hearers to repentance.' While this change is to be welcomed I still believe there is a need for recognized evangelists to enable the fulfilment of this ministry. This same need was expressed a hundred years ago when the Bishop of Lichfield reported on the Committee of Lay Evangelists and said, 'It is expedient that such recognition should be given by sending [evangelists] out with Episcopal authority.'[9]

The Office of Evangelist

Some may be surprised to find that the office of evangelist is recognized by canon law of the Church of England. Canon Law, 1967, E7.2 of lay workers says, 'A man or woman admitted to the Office of Evangelist is thereby admitted as a lay worker of the Church.' This has been interpreted to mean that only lay people can enter this office, but is this what it is really about? One has to know something of the background to understand why it was expressed in this form.

The development of the office of evangelist in the Church of England was part of the battle for a recognized lay ministry in the latter part of the nineteenth century. There were a number of lay ministries demanding some form of recognition, such as the brotherhoods of evangelists in Lichfield, Lincoln and Durham dioceses, the Church Pastoral Aid Society's Lay Assistants and Church Army evangelists. The outcome of all this was this was a resolution which reads:

'It is expedient in order to recognize a trained evangelist, and authorize him to perform the duties of his office in any Diocese, that the Bishop of the Diocese should grant him a "Reader's" licence in the form similar to that recommended in 1866.'[10]

The evangelist was to be admitted to the office of evangelist, an office akin to that of reader, in the diocese in which he was trained.[11] Church Army men, for example, were admitted to the office of evangelist in the diocese of London.[12]

A distinction between Reader and Evangelist was recognized. In discussions relating to a report of January 1896 from a Committee on Lay Evangelists it emerged that whereas the primary role of the reader was seen to be consolidation and working in one place, that of the evangelist was seen as the extension of God's kingdom with a greater mobility than that of a permanent assistant to clergy in one place, though both readers and evangelists

---

9 Chronicles of the Convocation of Canterbury, February 1895-96.
10 The Chronicles of Convocation Upper House, Report No 303, 1897.
11 Women were not admitted to the office of evangelist until 1962, but since 1921 Church Army Sisters had held the parallel office of Mission Sister.
12 The licence given in the London Diocese clearly specified the holder was an evangelist.

were recognized as having some pastoral responsibility.[13]

With the passage of time most of the other organisations ceased to train lay evangelists and the office of evangelist eventually became a Church Army monopoly. When the Church Army College moved from the London diocese in 1960s, a wider licence was given by the Archbishop of Canterbury which was affirmed by the bishop of the diocese in which the evangelists worked.

The office was, then, recognized by the Church of England canon law in the revision of 1967. At that stage only the lay evangelists of the Church Army held the office. The linking with a canon on lay ministry was a device to find a way of recognizing the office. Yet the way the office was so recognized appears, to some, to limit its scope. However, it is unlikely that such a thought was in the minds of those who formulated this revision to the law. They were simply describing the situation that existed at the time. Whatever the shortcomings of the legislation, the Church Army has kept the office of evangelist alive in the Church of England.

As part of the 1990s 'Decade of Evangelism' the discussion has been opened up again. In the meantime, however, some dioceses have found local ways of authorizing their own evangelists. Rochester's lay evangelists are 'commissioned.' Sheffield diocese plans a similar 'authorization' to that of lay pastoral workers. The Bishop of Southwell issues a 'Letter of Commendation' to gifted evangelists who live in the diocese and have undertaken some theological training.[14] In these cases authority is given by individual diocesan bishops. While these various devices offer recognition and authority, the picture is confusing. What is still required is some more general 'licence' accepted across the church and respected in every diocese.

Office or Order?

We have used the word 'office' in relation to evangelists. Is there then a difference between an office and an order? The Latin roots of the words do suggest some difference, order meaning 'rank' or 'position'[15] and office meaning 'function' or 'duty.'[16] In the ASB Ordinal, however, this distinction is blurred.[17] Perhaps there is a case for returning to the older distinction. If 'order' is taken to mean leadership, rank or position and 'office' understood as function, then we may have a similar distinction to the one between formal leadership and the charismatic ministry.[18]

---

13 Convocation Report No. 303
14 See 'Evangelists in the Diocese of Southwell,' a publicity brochure produced by the Southwell Diocese.
15 Latin: *ordo, ordinis.*
16 Latin: *officium, officii.*
17 The 1662 Book of Common Prayer retains something of this distinction.
18 The office of evangelist is an 'irregular' ministry like that of the OT prophet. The three fold ministry is 'regular.' ('The Office of the Evangelist,' Capt. Hutton, CA *Evangelistic Grindstones*, circa 1920, pp 62ff).

It appears that some people function as evangelists for a time and then take on another role, perhaps a pastoral one. There are others who begin as pastors and become evangelists. Being an evangelist seems to be about functioning in a particular way, that is, exercising the office. In that case, the role suits the concept of office better than that of order.

If I am right in arguing for a difference between order and office, then there is no reason why a person in holy orders should not also hold the office of an evangelist. There have been many ordained evangelists, yet some, at least, have found it necessary to shed the work of leading a congregation to enable them to exercise their evangelistic ministry. That is not to say that one cannot exercise some kind of evangelistic ministry while leading a church, and many clergy would see themselves as pastor-evangelists. Yet it does seem that the pastor-evangelist role is different from that of the evangelist. Perhaps this is something which needs to be recognized and clarified. The church leader's main concern will not be solely with evangelism and there is also the sheer problem of time. Can any clergy person in a normal parish role fulfil the role of an evangelist? It would seem that the pressures of leading a congregation persuade me to give a negative answer to the question. Ultimately even clergy evangelists need to be free to evangelize.

5

Deployment of Evangelists
in the Church of England

Given the fact that we have people with the gift of an evangelist, how can the Church of England set them free to do the work to which God has called them?

Parish Deployment

One of the main ways of deploying stipendiary evangelists has been in parishes. The strength of parish work is that they are able to operate within localities and communities which relate to the continuing mission of the Church of England. That said, there is always the problem that evangelists will find themselves too easily caught up in the maintenance structures of the church. However, this need not be the case. The Church Army parish evangelists' review of 1984 drew attention to the need for evangelists to have a clear purpose which focused on evangelistic tasks. Where this was the case they were contributing to the growth of the church.[19] All evangelists working in parishes, whether stipendiary or non-stipendiary, require a clear job description which will free them to function effectively. Clergy and church leaders need to understand what an evangelist's function is.

If parish evangelists are to have specific evangelistic tasks, what can these tasks include? Perhaps the most natural area of work is on the fringe of the church with people who come seeking help or those who look to the church for its occasional offices. Many parish evangelists have found this a fruitful area for potential new Christians through enquirers' groups. There are opportunities through church fringe groups like drop-in centres, parent and toddler groups and the like. In recent years there has been new growth through church planting and some evangelists have actually started more than one new church in a parish.

However, the present situation in the Church of England as reflected in *Ministry, A Pastoral Letter from the House of Bishops* leaves the future of the stipendiary lay parish evangelist in some doubt. While it draws attention to the importance of 'mission and active evangelism' it says it will be difficult for lay ministers of all kinds to find suitable appointments. This may leave room for some stipendiary clergy evangelists, but one cannot help feeling that the focus on clergy will lead to maintenance and pastoral priorities.

---

19 R W Canvin, *Report on the Church Army Parochial Evangelists Review 1984* (Limuru House, Christow, Exeter).

Yet three things are happening which may give some hope for the future. First, a number of Church Army evangelists are finding themselves licensed to work in a non-stipendiary capacity. Most of these have spouses whose work demands they live in a specific locality. They are qualified (by virtue of the ABM-assessed Church Army course) to be stipendiary, but their situation has demanded they find other ways of being an evangelist.

The second development is the training and commissioning of lay parish evangelists as in Rochester in 1994. The role of these lay parish evangelists is complementary and parallel to that of other recognized lay ministries like reader and pastoral assistant. They are expected to be part of the parish ministry team and their functions can include: visiting and leading visiting teams; speaking on informal occasions in worship; leading house groups for enquirers and helping seekers; stimulating mission at home and overseas; linking prayer with evangelism within the congregation; the ministry of welcome and hospitality; helping with special evangelistic services.[20] Sheffield has a similar scheme and the first evangelists are due to be authorized in January 1996.

Issues in Parish Deployment

Most of the questions which are being asked about the feasibility of these schemes have been asked before with respect to NSM clergy and other lay schemes like lay pastoral assistants. What happens, for example, if the evangelists move from the church to which they are authorized? Will they be allowed to exercise their evangelistic gift? Will people understand the nature of their role? The first question is an important one especially if, on the one hand, they are authorized to work mainly in the one parish, and on the other, as at present, there is no uniform authorization across dioceses. If they move to another diocese there may be no way the authorization can be transferred. Clearly, for the present, the actual authorization is limited and that must be understood from the beginning. Even within the diocese it will not follow that the new parish will want to take up the offer of the evangelist. Rochester diocese, wisely, suggests the possibility of people becoming members of a deanery team of evangelists and a diocesan fellowship of evangelists.

How people are used or valued in the local church is part of a wider issue of the development of leadership ministry teams in churches which include both clergy and lay, salaried and non-stipendiary. Where there is this kind of collaborative ministry (and surely this should be the aim of all churches) roles can be discussed and identified and support provided. As we know, many churches have not yet arrived at this position and so preparatory work

20 Michael Howard, 'Rochester's answer to the challenge of evangelism,' in *The Church of England Newspaper*, 2 September 1995.

has to be done.

Sheffield diocese facilitates the work of the lay parish evangelists in the following ways. No person joins the evangelist's course without the full support of incumbent and PCC. The training officer spends time with incumbents and PCCs to explain the nature of the ministry and how it relates to the continuing ministry of the church. There have also been a number of meetings at which the evangelists, their incumbents and the training team have met to talk though the implications of the evangelist's ministry in the local church.

Clearly, to have non-stipendiary lay people authorized as evangelists is a major step forward. There is relatively little financial outlay so there will be no limit to the number of evangelists a parish can have. These evangelists are not taken out of their own locality to train and then set to work in a place where they are not known. They can continue after authorization to work with the people they already know, utilizing their existing networks.

Everyday Evangelists

What kind of people, then, are being put forward by their church to be lay parish evangelists? Amy is a widow and a grandmother. She has been a Christian ten years and has a natural way of gossiping the gospel. A few years ago she felt her Christian life had come to a standstill and during that period was 'given a picture' of an open door. For her, this picture linked with an invitation to join the diocesan evangelist's training course. She is currently involved in evangelism in her parish as a member of the evangelism team.

Brian and Cathy are a married couple with teenage children. In spite of having a church background, they drifted away but eventually came into a living relationship with God just over ten years ago. Brian is also a reader. A few years ago they put together a gospel presentation with music through which they together share their story.

David is in his late thirties, single and a computer programmer. He has been a Christian for four years and came onto the parish evangelist's course at the vicar's suggestion. Also in the same parish is Elizabeth, a single mum with two young children. She also has been a Christian for four years and during that time has led Christian basics groups in the parish. Both David and Elizabeth are evangelism coordinators for the church and are involved in faith sharing and servant evangelism which includes cleaning cars and picking up litter.

Fred is head of Physical Education at a comprehensive school. Formerly he was a professional footballer until a back injury ended that career. He is married with two younger teenage children. He has been a Christian for over ten years and has been involved with children's and youth work in the church. He is concerned that some people attend church for a short while and then drift away. Churches, he thinks, ought to work harder at keeping these fringe contacts.

In giving these illustrations we connect with the examples offered at the beginning of this paper. These people have already shown some evangelism potential, but they seem not far removed from the ordinary run of church members. Churches need to notice the potential evangelists in their congregation.

There is, however, another route, which some parishes have taken. But first a story. A church wanted to appoint a trained and accredited lay-evangelist. It was prepared to pay the evangelist's salary and provide a house. Once negotiations started it was discovered that the appointment could not be made because the diocese already had its full quota of paid lay workers. Even though the church was prepared to cover the costs that appointment could not be made. Being an enterprising congregation they still went ahead and appointed a Bible College-trained stipendiary evangelist, but who is not 'recognized' as such outside of the local church. Can this be right when the Church's bureaucracy gets in the way of appointing accredited evangelists or of finding a way of recognizing all those who are stipendiary evangelists? This is not the only instance of such an appointment. In the present climate this is the only way open to some churches to add to their professional staff and, no doubt, these kinds of appointments will continue.

Deanery Evangelists

A few evangelists have been licensed to serve deaneries. The length of their stay varied from nine months to more than six or seven years. The deaneries they worked in represented a wide sociological mix from rural Norfolk to urban Leeds. Some of them pioneered new initiatives, helped with parish audits, stimulated church planting, became a focus for youth evangelism and developed seeker groups. Others were able to train a deanery faith sharing team to share the work with them. Such work, however, was not free from problems. There was no easy way of giving equal time to each parish and to attempt to do so was not practical. In fact, none of the evangelists actually claimed to have worked in all the parishes in the deanery, but they had been able, at times, to get all the churches involved in a deanery-wide project, like a training day or even a town mission.[21] In spite of the fact that they were officially licensed to work in the whole deanery, parochialism had remained one of the main problems they had to face.

Most of these projects were directly funded by the diocese with some help from deanery or voluntary funding. A recent appointment of a clergy evangelism enabler to a deanery was different. The deanery had been allo-

---

21 Information based on a survey of 11 deanery evangelists.

cated an extra clergy place due to population growth and so a decision was taken to appoint an evangelism enabler. Whatever the future of this particular project, the concept needs further consideration. In a deanery one of the allocated clergy places could be used for a full-time evangelist. Alternatively, the parishes may be persuaded to raise the funding between them.

Diocesan Appointments

Dioceses sometimes have appointed proven evangelists as Canon Missioner, without formally licensing them as evangelists. With the heightened awareness at the end of the twentieth century and the Decade of Evangelism most dioceses have a person specifically to lead the work of evangelism. Such people often, rightly, have a role more focused on training clergy and laity in evangelism. Yet the question remains whether they can be described as evangelists. At least two dioceses have formally recognized a few evangelists with a proven track record, mostly unpaid or self-supporting, to work across the diocese. Such a move is to be encouraged and one would want to see parallel developments elsewhere. If this practice were to be extended to other dioceses then, as suggested earlier, some kind of national accreditation should be made available to these people and others who are working at a national level.

Over the years the mission agencies and religious communities like the Franciscans, Community of the Resurrection and the Society of St John the Evangelist with their more focused objectives, have had a crucial role in deploying and supporting evangelists, in more flexible ways than the church has been able to do. The Church Army and the Church Pastoral Aid Society in particular employ evangelists to work over wider areas than diocese, deanery or parish. Will it be left for those with a national brief to be supported by religious communities, the mission agencies or their own private trust funds as is already happening? The overseas missionary societies are deploying resources in areas where there are ethnic communities. Leaving aside the issue of licensing and looking at the broader field of all mission and evangelistic agencies, it would appear that they have been the main agents for the deployment of evangelists.

There is quite a lot to encourage us, but one thing remains of concern. Should the Church of England continue to put most of its resources into the pastoral/priestly ministry? Can we not channel more of those resources into training, encouraging and deploying evangelists?

6
Developing the Evangelistic Gift

If we need to identify, enable and support evangelists, then we require a clearer idea of what is happening. Fifty evangelists filled in questionnaires relating to these aspects of their work, so perhaps we can note some trends within this sampling.[22]

Over 60% (31) said they were conscious of a call to do the work of an evangelist and a few others (5) mentioned a call to 'do something for God.' For a few the call came during a particular time of prayer, reflection, anointing of the Holy Spirit or of reading appropriate literature. Two said they were young, 12 or 15 years old, when the call first came. At least three entered into professional ministry with their denomination before they felt the particular call to evangelism.

60% (30) said they were involved in organized evangelistic activity at the time of their call and over 50% (27) said their evangelistic gift was recognized by others. For some of them this was the first time they had been aware of the gift. Those who identified the gift for them included parish clergy, a university chaplain, other evangelists, a house group leader and friends. 'My vicar couldn't believe I wanted to be a gardener all my life,' said one. In some instances the Diocesan Vocations Officer had recognized that the person had an evangelistic gift and not a pastoral one! Yet there were five others who did not have this kind of initial recognition.

Seeing it Happen

Two important things emerge. First, if 60% of the evangelists were involved in evangelistic activity when the call came to them, does this mean that a large percentage of evangelists are likely to come from churches where evangelistic activity is already taking place? What about those churches where evangelism has a low priority? We clearly need to encourage people to get involved in such activity if evangelists are going to emerge. If an opportunity to be involved in evangelism cannot be provided locally either the diocese or one of the evangelism agencies will be able to help. Second, almost as many were identified and encouraged as evangelists by church leaders or members and friends. What happens, then, in situations where church leaders are not clear what an evangelist is? Is there a need for church leaders and congregations to be taught to recognize the evangelistic gift?

Seven people said they simply witnessed to Christ and began to see

---

[22] Twenty-five were working mainly within the Church of England, 12 were Anglicans working with the wider Church and 13 were from other denominations.

people's lives changed; they were not aware of any call. They became evangelists as they discovered their witness was effective and people turned to Christ. It was a natural development without any specific call. They thought it was simply part of being a Christian. There were three others who were asked to speak at a meeting and in response did the work of an evangelist. One of these said, 'My first "appeal" was unusually successful.' Clearly we just have to let these things happen and support as necessary.

However, the ease with which the doors to evangelistic opportunity opened appear to have varied. Almost 60% (29) had no difficulty at all while almost 25% (12) found it hard to find ways forward. A few responses were mixed and many just carried on with the work of evangelism.

Those who experienced difficulty found this to be the case for a variety of reasons. One said that the replies from the groups he approached lacked enthusiasm and only a personal intervention of an evangelist enabled him to get an interview. Three said they considered ordination but it was not the right way for them. One of these said it seemed it was either youth work or ordination and neither seemed right for him. Yet at least seven of those who replied were ordained. Certain categories of people had initial difficulty because of their background, disability or being a divorcee.

People initially developed their gifts further in a number of ways. They obviously needed opportunities to get on with evangelism. 'The local church was very supportive in helping me.' 'I was given a job description to suit my gifts.' 'I took voluntary work with Manchester City Mission.' 'There were lots of opportunities in the local church.' 'I was too busy to worry about it.' 'I was involved in schools work (pre-evangelism).' Some said they used the gift in whatever place they were as well as in the local church. One said he went forward by trial and error. One undertook a two-year training course with London City Mission; another found opportunities at Scargill House. Yet another person worked in the crypt at St. George's, Leeds, which he claimed helped him see the context of evangelism, while another was involved with ministry with the deaf. Evangelistic agencies also provided opportunities for people to practice evangelism. A further person took time to study the theology of how children and youth find faith.

Over 60% (32) said they had good support from their local church, though two others said it took time in coming. Two said their churches were cautious, but encouraged them to test their call. Yet, sadly, two others said the local church did not show any interest at all and they had to find the help they needed elsewhere. Clearly, initial support from the local church is crucial. The comments about training were mixed. Some (3) who had been through a professional ministry training found the course lacking in evangelistic content. One said 'No, nothing at college (amazingly)!' and another 'I went to a college which had no course on evangelism.' However, they had been able to take advantage of various conferences and training days they had come across. Those who entered the Church Army or Cliff College found a ready-made residential course. One who had three months at a Bible college said that the real training came later when he worked for three years with an evangelist. Three people mentioned that training was available through the lay evangelists scheme which their diocese was running, but until the scheme was set up they had picked up what they could at the various training days on offer. Others (4) mentioned training with interdenominational evangelistic agencies.

There is not space to comment in detail about training, but some things can be said. Courses for training people to be evangelists need to be much more available with a variety of degrees of depth depending on the evangelist and what they need to know and experience. Working alongside evangelists and watching them at work was mentioned by four as important for them. 'Training on the job' was mentioned by both a Roman Catholic priest and an evangelist from a house church. Others simply spoke about being involved with various evangelistic groups and 'learning by doing.' This practical element in training cannot be ignored.

7

Evangelists, Church Structures and Recognition

Does the evangelist have a liturgical function? Part of the problem in trying to answer this question lies within Anglican understandings of the roles of clergy and laity. Are there aspects of ministry which are currently the monopoly of the ordained ministry which may form part of the evangelist's work? These days there does not seem to be any serious reason why accredited lay people should not baptize, and evangelists may sometimes expect to baptize their own converts. Further, an integral part of evangelism is the proclamation of the forgiveness of sins. Formally, within the Anglican church this is the prerogative of the ordained. Yet there is a good case for any member of the church offering forgiveness to others (Matt 6.14-15; James 5.13-18) and this ministry is basic to the spread of the good news (Luke 24.46-47; John 20.22-23). Surely the formal ministry of the forgiveness of sins is integral to the role of the evangelist, whether clergy or lay.

There is, however, another area which needs some revision. If a church-planting evangelist is creating a new congregation is it not right that the congregation should participate in the eucharist from the beginning? Is it right that it has to wait until it is a 'proper' church with its own 'proper' minister before it has a eucharistic ministry? Some, no doubt, would feel the only way the Anglican church could resolve the situation is by ordaining all church planting evangelists. However, another answer would be to recognize that the situation was provisional and provide some temporary arrangements. After all, we are thinking of the time in the life of a church before order has been fully developed. The leader of the group whether lay or ordained would be the proper person to celebrate communion, an idea propounded some years ago by both Bishop J B Lightfoot and Roland Allen.[23]

There is also another issue. How long does a church planting evangelist remain with the church plant? As far as the Acts of the Apostles is concerned, once the church was established the apostle or evangelist appears to have moved on. Would ordaining church planting evangelists confuse their role?

Recognition and Training

Does the evangelist's role demand more recognition? Evangelists are often seen as second rate alongside pastors/presbyters. Also, in an episcopal church clergy are perceived to have more status than lay people. The lay evangelist loses out on both counts. This has led some to argue that a reordered diaconate which was no longer seen as a step prior to ordination could provide an 'order' for evangelists. It is doubtful whether the diaconate will ever be perceived as anything other than a clerical order and to put all evangelists into one order will, no doubt, prove restricting. Evangelists cannot be put neatly into the church's pigeon holes.

This lack of recognition is sometimes reflected in attitudes to training. A group of senior African church leaders were explaining their denomination's ministerial training programme. For the accredited evangelist there is a three year training programme. After a further two years' training the evangelist became a pastor. In this situation evangelists are seen as pastors in the making. Yet such a view is not restricted to Africa. Why is it often thought that pastors require more or better training than evangelists? Surely evangelists are a complementary and equal ministry to that of other ministries and recognition and quality of training should reflect this.

There are good things happening in the Church of England. A number of dioceses are beginning to identify, train and enable evangelists. The voluntary societies are continuing to train and enable evangelists. But questions remain. Are evangelists an integral part of Anglican ministry? If so, can we put more resources into enabling and supporting them? Can we find an appropriate way of accrediting them which will be recognized throughout the Church of England? The challenge to the Church is to provide the necessary support which will set them free to be what evangelists should be.

---

23 J B Lightfoot, *The Epistle of St Paul to the Philippians*, (MacMillan, 1891); Roland Allen,
'The Priesthood of the Church,' in *Church Quarterly Review*, January 1933.